My Pet

DOG

Kate Petty

Stargazer Books

Dogs as pets

Dogs have lived with humans for over 10,000 years. A wild dog often lives in a pack and obeys the pack leader. A tame dog needs its owner to be its leader.

Dogs need to be properly fed and exercised but they also need lots of love. Most big dogs live for eight to ten years but some smaller ones can live to be 14 or 15.

The German Shepherd dog looks very much like its wolflike ancestor.

As if they were in a pack, these Border Collie pups fight for leadership. ▶

All kinds of dogs

Dogs come in more different shapes and sizes than any other animal. This is because they have been bred for so many different uses—from pulling sleds to sitting on laps.

Some breeds make better pets than others and some of the nicest pets have no pedigree at all. Dogs like this, which are a mixture of breeds, are called mongrels.

Old English Sheepdog

Pomeranian

Bulldog

This mongrel's happy expression shows that it is a well-loved family pet. ▶

About dogs

You can tell how a dog is feeling by its large, soulful eyes and its expressive tail. Many dogs have thick, hairy coats to keep out the cold, and very strong, pointed teeth for eating meat.

A dog's sense of smell is a thousand times stronger than ours. Their hearing is much better too. They can hear higher pitched sounds than humans can.

Dogs prick up their ears like this at the slightest sound.

A Beagle always follows the scent of other animals.

It is easy to see that this Golden Retriever is happy and healthy. ▶

Running and jumping

In the wild, dogs have to run quickly to catch their fast moving prey. Most dogs are powerful runners. The Greyhound is very fast and can run at 32 mph (52 km/h).

A Greyhound, too, holds the long jump record of more than 30 feet (9m). Many dogs can jump well. German Shepherds have been known to jump over obstacles 11 feet (3m) high.

Border Collies take fences in their stride when they round up sheep.

Greyhounds need wide-open spaces for stretching their legs. ▶

Eating

All dogs are meat-eaters, but they need cereal too. Dogs' appetites vary according to their size and the amount of exercise they take. A Great Dane eats around 2.2 pounds (one kilo) of meat and cereals each day.

Growing puppies need more food than adult dogs and should be fed three times a day. Adult dogs will often eat just once a day but should always have plenty of water to drink.

A small puppy needs to eat off a plate.

A large drinking bowl for a large Great Dane. ▶

Who wants to fight?

As a pack animal, a dog needs to know who's boss. It will snarl and bare its teeth if it feels threatened by a strange dog. Some breeds of dogs are naturally more aggressive than others.

When two dogs meet they might start to fight. But usually the weaker—or more friendly—dog will show submission by sitting back and flattening its ears. Or it might roll on to its back.

The Corgi puppy shows the Jack Russell that it doesn't want to fight.

Dogs learn a lot about each other by sniffing and rubbing noses. ▶

Our best friend

Most dogs are highly intelligent. They are better at learning than any other animal. They respond to good teaching with affection and loyalty.

Dogs enjoy working. They help us in many ways as police dogs, sniffer dogs, retrievers, and guard dogs. How would a sheep farmer manage without his dogs?

Labradors make reliable guide dogs for the blind.

The English Setter puppy waits to be rewarded for fetching the scarf. ▶

Newborn puppies

Puppies are quite helpless when they are born. It is about three days before they can hear and two weeks before they can see.

Puppies will start to stagger around at three and a half weeks, but by eight weeks they can usually feed themselves and are ready to leave their mother. They are still babies, though, and need many hours of sleep and several meals a day.

This puppy has only just been born.

You can still see the umbilical cord which joined it to its mother.

This patient Retriever will feed her enormous litter of puppies for about five weeks. ▶

Growing up

Puppies have lots to learn and their owners need patience. Some smaller breeds are fully grown at six months but larger dogs might take two years to reach their full size.

Puppies get their baby teeth at two to three weeks. Their permanent teeth come through at about four months and they need to be given plenty of things to chew on.

The King Charles Spaniel puppy is still a baby who makes mistakes.

These Collie pups are teething. Luckily, they have found some old rope to chew on. ▶

Out and about

All dogs need daily exercise and play to keep them fit and healthy. The city dog has to be well trained so that it is not a nuisance to other people or a danger to traffic.

Good training is just as important to the country dog. As well as road sense, it has to learn respect for the other animals it will meet in the fields and woods.

This West Highland Terrier thinks it is time for a walk.

A Black Pug exercising with its Old English Sheepdog friend ▶

Know your dogs

This chart will help you recognize some of the different breeds of dogs. A dog show is the best place to see them all, but the local park on a Sunday afternoon is almost as good!

Dogs vary in every way. It is strange to think that the 150-pound (68-kg) Saint Bernard and the 6-pound (3-kg) Yorkshire Terrier share the same ancestors.

Irish Wolfhound

Whippet

Boxer

English Springer Spaniel

Toy Poodle

Afghan
Hound

Yorkshire
Terrier

Saint
Bernard

Dalmation

Dachshund

23

Index

©Aladdin Books Ltd 2006

Produced by
Aladdin Books Ltd

First published in the
United States in 2006 by
Stargazer Books
c/o The Creative Company
123 South Broad Street
P.O. Box 227
Mankato, Minnesota 56002

Designer: Pete Bennett – PBD
Editor: Rebecca Pash
Illustrator: George Thompson
Picture Research: Cee Weston-Baker

Printed in Malaysia

Photographic credits:
Cover: PBD; pages 3, 5, 13 19 & 21:
Bruce Coleman; pages 7, 9, 11, 15 & 17:
Sally Anne Thompson/Animal
Photography

*Library of Congress Cataloging-in-
Publication Data*

Petty, Kate.
  Dog / by Kate Petty.
    p. cm. -- (My pet)
  Includes index.
  ISBN 1-59604-026-2 (alk. paper)
    1. Dogs--Juvenile literature. I. Title.

SF426.5.P457 2005
636.7--dc22
                            2004063333